SKYSCRAPERS

MASTERPIECES
OF ARCHITECTURE

CHARLES SHEPPARD

SMITHMARK

This edition published in 1996 by SMITHMARK Publishers,
a division of U.S. Media Holdings, Inc., 16 East 32nd Street, New York, NY 10016.

SMITHMARK books are available for bulk purchase for sales promotion and premium use.
For details write or call the manager of special sales,
SMITHMARK Publishers, 16 East 32nd Street, New York, NY 10016; (212) 532-6600.

This book was designed and produced by Todtri Productions Limited
P.O. Box 572, New York, NY 10116-0572 FAX: (212) 279-1241

Printed and bound in Singapore

Library of Congress Catalog Card Number 96-68166
ISBN 0-7651-9940-8

Author: Charles Sheppard

Publisher: Robert M. Tod
Book Designer: Mark Weinberg
Production Coordinator: Heather Weigel
Senior Editor: Edward Douglas
Project Editor: Cynthia Sternau
Editorial Consultant: Hilary Scannell
Assistant Editor: Linda Greer
Picture Researcher: Natalie Goldstein
Typesetting: Command-O, NYC

PICTURE CREDITS

CONTENTS

THE STORY OF THE SKYSCRAPER

In 1873, the French novelist Jules Verne sent his hero Phileas Fogg "around the world in eighty days," an adventure celebrating the new opportunities of mechanized travel by steamship and railway. Fogg only succeeded in claiming his bet with the aid of the international date line—eighty days was then a realistic technical limit.

A more relaxed tourist leaving Paris at the same time, and taking fifteen years to marvel at the wonders of the world, would have seen nothing on all his travels so remarkable as the sight greeting him on the Champs de Mars in Paris on his return in 1889. The elegant curves of the skeletal tower designed by French engineer Alexandre-Gustav Eiffel for the great Paris Exhibition of 1889 have become an instantly recognizable symbol of Paris, indeed of France itself. Eiffel also built great stations and bridges, and devised the structure for the Statue of Liberty in New York harbor, but his name is rightly immortalized by this prototype skyscraper.

Our world-weary traveler would first have been struck by the sheer height of the Eiffel Tower, for at 984 feet (300 meters), it was almost double the height of any previous structure. The bare ironwork and exposed structural frame would also have been noticible, but these features were not new. The Kew Gardens Palm House in London (Burton and Turner, 1844) pioneered iron framing and glass infill. The Crystal Palace, Sir Joseph Paxton's Great Exhibition Hall in London (1851), used standardized iron and glass components repeated over and over to form a huge building. Eiffel's contribution was to rivet together small, standard iron sections to form large, three-dimensional girders, giving maximum strength for the minimum weight. The tower showed that tall structures could be built of iron or steel at a small fraction of the weight of the equivalent masonry.

The ride up the Eiffel Tower to the viewing platforms would have been another new experience for the average visitor. Elevators in buildings were still a novelty—but without them few people would have managed the climb to the top. With its new technologies the Eiffel Tower pointed the way forward—it was a true *"tour de force."*

RIGHT: Designed by French engineer Alexandre-Gustav Eiffel for the great Paris Exhibition of 1889, the elegant curves of the Eiffel Tower have come to symbolize the spirit of France.

FOLLOWING PAGE:
In 1976, the monolithic twin towers of the World Trade Center, at 1,350 feet (411 meters), became New York City's tallest buildings.

LEFT: Built in 1975, Toronto's CN Tower is one of a new breed of telecommunications skyscrapers, but in form it resembles the famous Tour de Beurre of Rouen.

RIGHT: A detail of the gorgeous ornamental facade from the Woolworth Building, which was quickly dubbed the "Cathedral of Commerce" by local media.

LEFT: The Cathedral of Notre Dame in Rouen, with its notable Tour de Beurre (butter tower). Rouen has been an archiepiscopal see since the fifth century and is especially rich in ecclesiastical buildings.

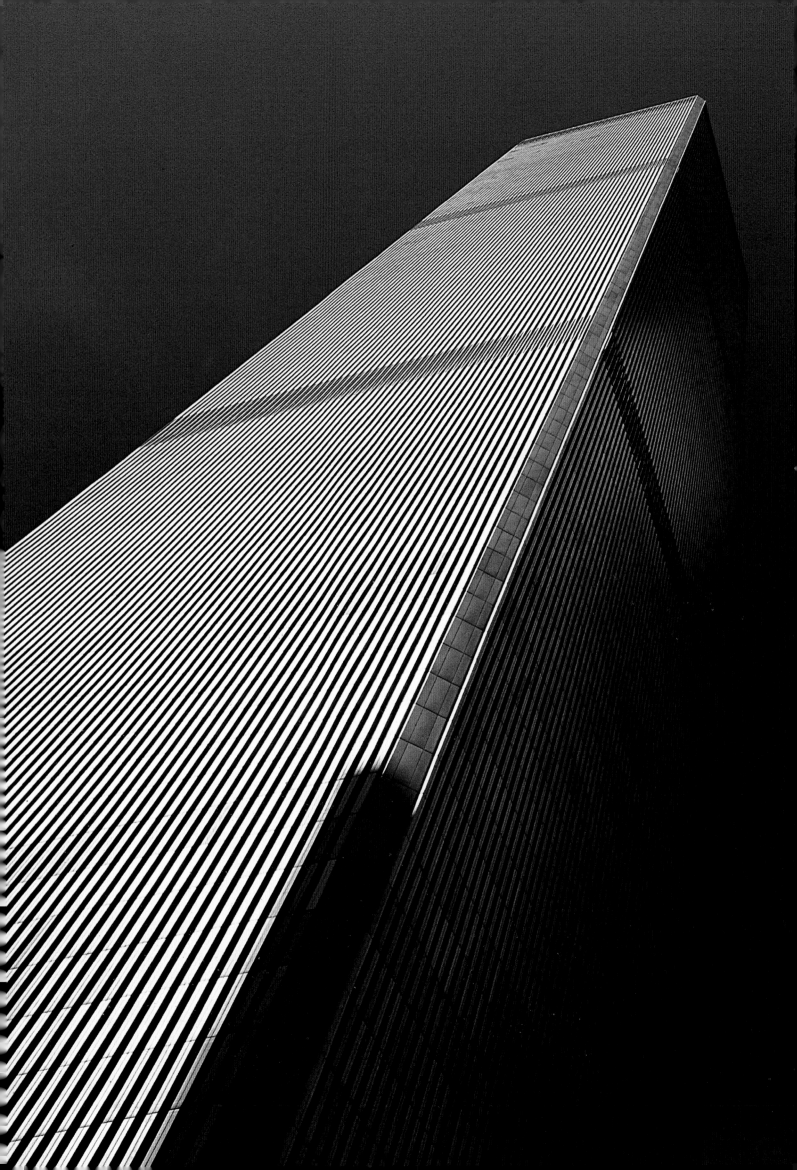

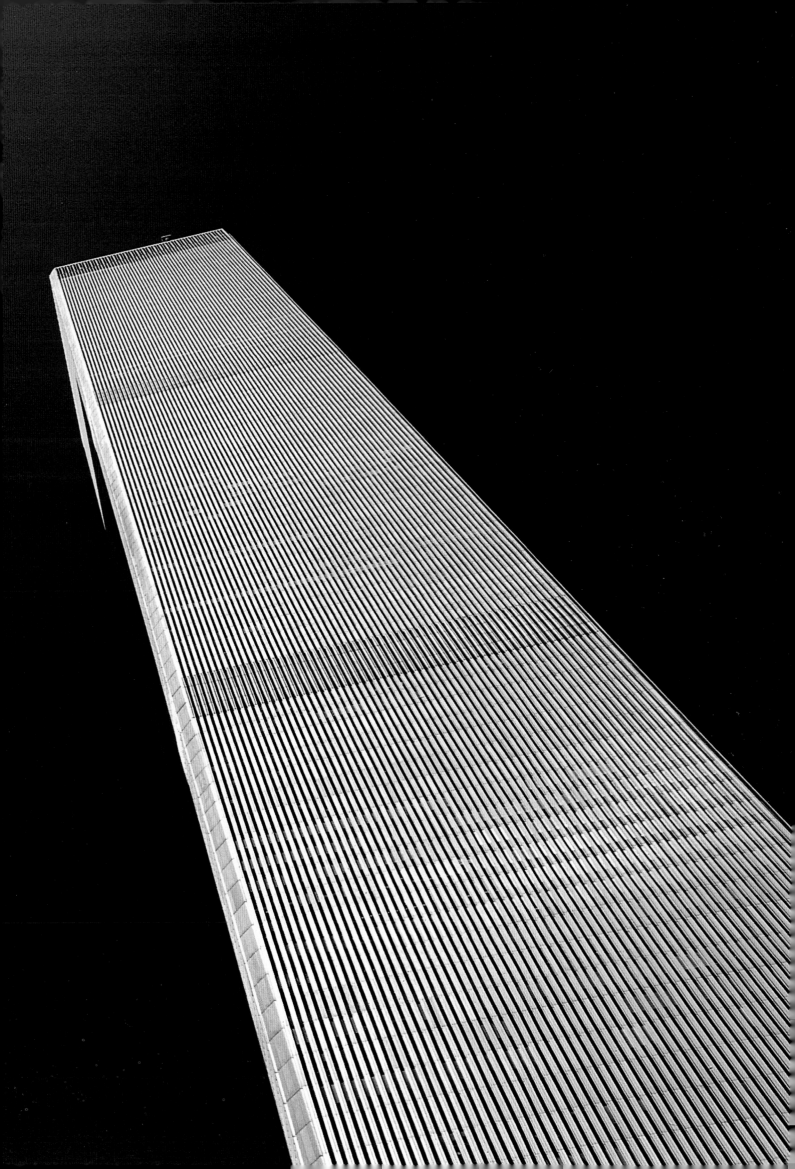

CHAPTER ONE

FROM THE PYRAMIDS TO THE EIFFEL TOWER

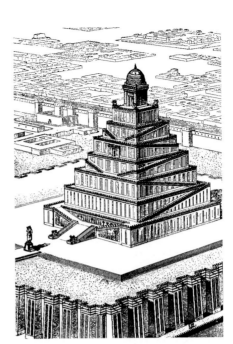

ABOVE: The Ziggurat of Ur, built by King Ur-Nammu , c. 2060 B.C. The ancient Mesopotamian ziggurat was square in plan, and built up in receding terraces.

In 1889, there were few buildings more than six or seven stories tall, and still fewer not built of masonry (brick or stone). Timber had to be used for roofs and floors where its tensile strength—resistance to being stretched—was essential; but after catastrophic fires, such as that in London in 1666, wood was prohibited for use in external walling within built-up areas in the center of towns.

So, until 1880, buildings in towns were constrained by the properties of masonry—principally by its weight. The higher a wall, the more it weighs, and the thicker its base has to be to support the load from above. In other words, a pyramid shape is required. Above a certain height it becomes cheaper to provide space in a lower, more extended building than to add an extra floor at the top.

Without elevators, there is a further limit to the number of floors in a building—three to four flights of stairs was traditionally considered enough. The grand palaces of Europe, built from 1300 to 1800, all had their principal rooms on the first and second floors, with domestic offices at ground level and servants living on the top floors or in attics.

Throughout history people have sought to build high. Asked why he wished to climb Mount Everest before his death on the mountain in 1924, the English adventurer George Mallory replied, "Because it is there." The urge to build high can perhaps in essence only be explained in a similar way—as a response to a challenge.

"Skyscrapers" of the Ancient World

The first of the Seven Wonders of the Ancient World, the Great Pyramid of Cheops at Gizeh in Egypt, may be described as the earliest attempt at a skyscraper (2700 B.C.). There are earlier pyramids, but this is the largest, and even today it remains one of the biggest and heaviest structures ever built.

If not a skyscraper in shape, the Great Pyramid has held the world's height record for longer than anything else built by man. Its base is 756 feet (230 meters) square—double the area of St. Peter's Cathedral in Rome. Its sides form almost exact equilateral triangles; the four faces, facing to the points of the compass, are therefore inclined at about 52 degrees to the ground. The top blocks are now missing, but the height would originally have been a staggering 482 feet (147 meters).

The labor of quarrying and shaping each of the two million stone blocks (at an average weight of 2 tons), transporting them by barge down the Nile, and placing the material in position defies imagination. The pyramids were in fact gigantic tombs; they stand as symbols of the pharaohs' divine aspirations and hopes of resurrection, as well, of course, of their temporal wealth and power.

The pyramid form is found elsewhere in the ancient world. There is only archaeological evidence of the Mesopotamian ziggurats (pyramids with wide steps forming terraces). The Hanging Gardens of Babylon, the Second Wonder of the Ancient World, would have been the most spectacular, and Babylon is reputed to have boasted 250 defensive towers on its walls. In Mexico, the Aztecs built pyramids of a similar shape.

LEFT: The Great Pyramid of Cheops at Gizeh, near Cairo, is the largest pyramid ever built. Dating from 2680 B.C., this astonishing edifice may aptly be described as the world's earliest attempt at a skyscraper.

The Pharos, or lighthouse, at Alexandria was the third of the Seven Wonders, and it is closer to the modern concept of a skyscraper. Built between 283 and 247 B.C. by Sosnatus of Cnidus, it stood 466 feet (142 meters) tall until its collapse in 1326 A.D.

The Romans turned their considerable engineering skills to building bridges, roads, and other practical forms (the Colosseum, although 160 feet [49 meters] tall, is not a sky-scraper in concept). They also built triumphal edifices such as Trajan's Column in Rome, which is 20 feet (6 meters) square at its base and has a diameter of about 15 feet (4.5 meters) above, rising 135 feet (41 meters) to the plinth of the Emperor.

Naturally this column symbolized the Emperor's importance and status—if not yet a god living in the sky, at least he was pointing in the right direction. Trajan's Column is a genuine building, not just a pillar: it is hollow, with thin walls and a staircase.

Later eras built their own wonders. The Jain and Hindu temples of India, such as those at Khajutaho (about 950 A.D.) and Tanjore (constructed in the fourteenth century) have a strong vertical emphasis; so does the late-eighteenth-century Temple of Dawn, at Wat Arun in Thailand. Chinese pagodas built from the fourteenth to the eighteenth centuries also orig-inated as religious buildings.

ABOVE: A step-pyramid from Chichén Itzá, an ancient Mayan city in Yucatan, Mexico. The Mayan pyramids, built in steep, receding blocks, were topped by ritual chambers, and, in some cases, possessed interior tomb crypts.

RIGHT: Set on a tiny island in the bay, the Pharos of Alexandria was built in the third cen-tury B.C. Constructed of white marble and designed by architect Sostratus the Cnidian, this famous lighthouse was known as one of the Seven Wonders of the World, and the fires burning on the top of the tower could be seen at a distance of one hundred miles.

ABOVE: Toulouse was an artistic and literary center of medieval Europe, and among the many outstanding buildings in that city is the romanesque Basilica of St. Sernin, an aesthetic ancestor of New York's Woolworth Building.

Pointing Toward Heaven

Medieval Europe was dominated by religion and the Church. Each community displayed its religious zeal, abetted by civic rivalry, in the size and height of its church. In their enthusiasm to achieve the highest possible vaulted ceilings and towers, the stonemasons and masterbuilders pushed stone technology to its limits, and beyond. In England, Salisbury Cathedral (1220–1255) is archetypal: over the crossing, an elegant spire

rises to more than 400 feet (123 meters) above the ground, pointing the way to heaven.

Although some French cathedrals such as Chartres have splendid external towers, the builders were preoccupied with the high vaulted ceiling, perfected at Amiens (1220–1288); this was 140 feet (43 meters) tall. At 158 feet (48 meters), the ceiling at Beauvais was the highest in Europe; but the builders had overreached themselves. The choir roof collapsed in 1284, and was reconstructed in 1337–1347; and the 500-foot-tall (150-meter) open-work spire over the transept/choir crossing, not buttressed by a nave, collapsed in 1573. In Belgium, Antwerp Cathedral has a magnificent western tower 400 feet (122 meters) tall, while in Germany the fifteenth-century Tower of Ulm stands 529 feet (161 meters) tall.

In fourteenth-century Gothic buildings, glass gradually replaced all stonework superfluous to structural requirements. These later churches almost achieve a framed construction—in stone. But this was an idea whose time had not yet come; it had to wait for a later century and a new material.

Rival political and religious factions and the patchwork of city-states in medieval Italy again produced fierce civic rivalry, expressed in the building of watchtowers to guard against enemies, and bell towers to warn the citizens against attack or

summon them to defend the city. In 1261, the torrazzo at Cremona, at 400 feet (122 meters), was the highest tower in existence. The best-known and most influential tower is the campanile, or bell tower, of St. Mark's Cathedral in Venice (now rebuilt in exactly its old form after a collapse in 1902). In the small Tuscan town of San Gimignano, Guelph–Ghibelline rivalries seem to have been eclipsed by the internal rivalries of the citizens. Each faction built a defensive tower keep, and aimed to outdo the others by building even higher. Of the original seventy-two towers in San Gimignano, only fourteen remain. But the narrow streets lined with palaces and overshadowed by towers still uncannily presage the modern centers of American cities.

Numerous folly towers were built in Europe between the seventeenth and nineteenth centuries to gratify the personal whims of landowners. The tower at Little Berkhamstead in Hertfordshire, England, is said to have been built in 1789 to allow Admiral Stratton a view of the flags on his merchant ships as they sailed up the Thames, so that he could ride into town in time to meet them. The flamboyant May's Folly in Hadlow, Kent, has no such apparent pretensions to utility.

Some towers were built solely for functional purposes—among them martello towers (forts built to withstand Napoleon's expected naval bombardments), shot towers (from which molten lead was poured from the top to form spherical pellets for gun cartridges), and massive stone lighthouses with their interlocking masonry constructed to withstand formidable storms.

In the nineteenth century, tall buildings were still constrained by age-old construction techniques and materials, despite two hundred years of mathematical and engineering advances. Big Ben, designed by Augustus Northmore Pugin in London in 1853, is a neo-Gothic reworking of the medieval Italian campanile. At 316 feet (96 meters) it dominates the whole Westminster complex, especially when viewed from across the Thames, and was intended to signify the heart of the greatest empire in the world.

The contrast between Big Ben and Eiffel's metal skeleton is striking: One looks back to the eras of masonry and its limitations, while the other boldly confronts the new age and the unknown.

BELOW: At the heart of Venice in St. Mark's Square, the tenth-century campanile of St. Mark's Cathedral is a pure spire reaching up toward heaven.

LEFT: Although its influence was firmly denied by architect Napoleon Le Brun, the tower addition to the Metropolitan Life Company Building in New York is remarkably similar in form to the campanile of St. Mark's Cathedral in Venice.

ABOVE: A view from across the River Thames of Big Ben and the Houses of Parliament, London. Of perpendicular Gothic design, the Westminster complex was built to replace an assortment of older building destroyed by fire in 1834.

The American Ethos

It was to be the New World, not the Old, that developed the potential of new materials and technologies into the huge structures that have transformed twentieth-century cities. In Europe, the architectural styles of the past had proclaimed the power of princes, church, and state. The United States was founded on the pursuit of liberty, both religious and civil. Its fine churches and large houses expressed wealth, not class.

For over two hundred years American buildings had followed successive styles in Europe, often giving them a New-World twist—for example, the Colonial timber houses of New England came to form their own unique brand of classicism. But by the 1870s, some American architects felt they should be producing an all-American architecture rather than slavishly following the example of Europe, where many of them had studied their professions.

European architects were too well aware of the heritage of their buildings and the cities which had evolved organically

over centuries. The early American cities along the East Coast also had fine historic centers, but as railways opened up the continent, new cities were built on open land where the past exerted less of a hold. Such cities provided the ideal opportunity for a break with tradition.

The nineteenth-century Industrial Revolution had produced a new wealthy class—the factory owners or entrepreneurs who, in Europe, had to jockey for status with the great institutions of state and church, and the inherited wealth of princes and landed aristocrats. But in the more egalitarian United States, these rich men became patrons. In the new cities they were able to give free expression to their pride and ambitions without European inhibitions.

The Chicago School

Chicago was founded by the railways—it was the great junction for all the lines in the Midwest. Founded on internal rather than overseas trade, this city was less influenced than New York by European styles and fashions. In 1871 fire ravaged the existing city and bigger buildings were needed to replace them. The central areas of cities such as Chicago, close to the railway stations, had acquired immense commercial value, so new buildings simply had to be as big as possible to maximize the financial returns of construction. Progressive designers seized the opportunity to develop building techniques utilizing the strength of iron—if iron railroads had created the city, should not its buildings also use iron?

By now iron had been used in engineering for a century, and for exhibition halls and railway stations for thirty to forty years; but it had still found no place in real architecture. Architects on both sides of the Atlantic had been too preoccupied with reworking the building styles of past eras to take iron, or later steel, seriously.

Two masonry buildings in New York reached a height of ten stories: George Post's Western Union Building (1875) and Richard Hunt's Tribune Building (1876). This was as tall as masonry structures could go. In Chicago, Burnham and Root's Montauk Block (1881–1882), often called the first skyscraper, reached 130 feet (40 meters). Its facades, unusually devoid of ornament, were the first example of the commercial style to be developed in the city.

Since the 1850s a number of factories and warehouses had been built with their internal walls replaced by a grid of iron

ABOVE: A 1929 photograph of the Tacoma Building at LaSalle & Madison Streets, Chicago, built in 1887-88 by Holabird & Roche, a pioneering architectural firm of the Chicago School.

RIGHT: The Home Insurance Company Building, (Chicago, 1884–1885) was the first building in the world to employ steel skeleton construction and embodied the general characteristics of a modern skyscraper.

THE CHICAGO BUILDING OF THE HOME INSURANCE CO.

OF NEW YORK

columns. Chicago architect William Le Baron Jenney adopted this structure for his first Leiter Building (1879). In the Home Insurance Company Building (Chicago, 1884–1885) he further extended the iron frame into the external walls to take a high proportion of their loading. The walls could now be thinner, with more, and larger windows—an important feature for a major downtown shopping area.

Jenney understood that in a framed building the outside walls need not carry any floor or roof loading—they could either be self-supporting or carried on the frame itself, floor by floor. His second Leiter Building (1889–1891) was fully framed, and for the first time in history buildings were freed from the shackling constraints of masonry.

The pioneering iron engineering works used cast iron, which has a high carbon content and good resistance to rust. Wrought iron has a lower carbon content, but a higher tensile strength, and was used for the early frames. Steel processing

removes more carbon and substitutes nickel, chrome, or manganese (depending on the type of steel required). Even by the 1890s the early steels of the late nineteenth century had achieved a much higher tensile strength than iron or timber. Bradford Gilbert's tower on lower Broadway (1889) was the first steel-framed building in New York.

Framed Structures/New Technologies

Wind loading was little understood, as were the means of resisting it. In the early 1890s, it had been noticed that rather than merely swaying in response to gusts, some framed structures had developed a regular oscillating sway—the building was storing the energy of the wind. This potential danger needed a solution before buildings could grow taller. In later buildings, bracing members were incorporated into the structure, transmitting the horizontal wind forces by these diagonals to the columns, and so to the ground.

ABOVE: Fashions change along with the skyline, and the Home Insurance Company Building in Chicago, a trendsetter in its time (1884–1885) was demolished in 1931 to make way for a more modern structure.

ABOVE: Built by D. H. Burnham and J. W. Root, the same architects who created the Monadnock Building, the Reliance Building in Chicago (1891–1894) used a steel skeleton frame, permitting an increase in the size of the windows.

With a real framed structure, windows could be much larger—and all the external walls other than the frame could be glass. This yielded better lit, more useful interiors, especially at ground level, where new, taller buildings were increasingly overshadowing the streets.

The sixteen-story Monadnock Building (D. H. Burnham and J. W. Root, 1889–1891) is of load-bearing external masonry, massive and undecorated. The windows are probably as large as they could be, and the walls at the base are 6 feet (1.8 meters) thick. The 1891–1894 Reliance Building, of similar height and by the same firm, illustrates the changes in window size permitted by a skeleton frame. It is a pointer to the future—a genuine prototype skyscraper. Another pioneering Chicago firm, Holabird and Roche, developed glazed facades more fully in their South Michigan Avenue facades of 1899.

Fire was still the greatest hazard to a building and its occupants. London had been the first city to enforce codes of practice relating to safety and the spread of fire after the conflagration in 1666. After Chicago's 1871 fire, designers were forced to protect the building frames. Iron and steel melt at relatively low temperatures—they could not otherwise be forged or cast. To prevent the collapse of the structural frame, it had to be protected with heat-resistant brick or terra-cotta tiles. Adequate escape routes were also needed, so the building was subdivided into a number of fire-resistant compartments, much like the watertight compartments of an ocean liner. There had to be more than one means of escape—stairs as well as elevators—in case people were cut off from one exit by fire.

Walking up more than five flights of stairs was not considered practical, so to grow upwards buildings needed elevators. Steam-powered hydraulic elevators and hoists were a proven technology. The problem was safety—there would be a disaster if the rope broke. In 1854, Elisha Graves Otis demonstrated a device in which a sprung-metal member attached to the pulling or carrying ropes would snap into notched side rails in the event of failure. The V. Haughnort and Company store in New York was then able install the world's first public elevator in 1857. The 130-foot-tall (40-meter) Equitable Building in New York (Gilman, Kendall and Post, 1870) was the first office building to boast an elevator.

In September of 1882, the Edison Electric Lighting Company switched on the lights in New York. Many other cities quickly followed suit and installed a gridded supply of electricity. Electric lighting and power transformed more than just street lighting, they altered the whole way buildings were lit and serviced. In 1889, the first electric elevator was installed in New York's Demarest Building. Air conditioning systems could now be developed, although at first these were primitive. Finally,

BELOW: The Monadnock Building (1889–1891) was constructed using load-bearing external masonry; the walls at the base are 6 feet (1.8 meters) thick.

telephones enabled workers in large offices to communicate easily with each other and with the outside world.

So the skyscraper, as it was beginning to be called, was the offspring of a complex set of interdependent technologies including steel, electricity, fire control, telecommunications, and elevators. Buildings were now far more complex than they had even been before.

But there is more to architecture than the mere provision of space. The new Chicago buildings were breaking with the traditions of their European predecessors by using iron and steel and a frame structure to double the number of floors. These also broke new ground in expressing frame in the building facades,

making a virtue of minimal decoration. The Monadnock Building even omits projecting windows sills. This style, whose exponents later became known as the Chicago School, was criticized at the time for being merely functional—not real architecture at all. However, there was one Chicago architect who was able, with delicate, restrained decoration, to make this uncompromising type of building not just publicly acceptable, but widely acclaimed. His name was Louis Sullivan.

Louis Sullivan

The first important buildings to be designed by Louis Sullivan (1856–1924) were Chicago's Auditorium Building and the Garrick Theater, both in the late 1880s. Without totally espousing the dictate that "form follows function," Sullivan took a building's structure as the starting point for a restrained style of decoration which was intended to emphasize and complement both materials and form.

Perhaps his finest achievement is the ten-story Wainwright Building (St. Louis, 1886–1890) which has the proportions of a near cube. The frame allows large windows, and is expressed with tall, thin pilasters laid flat on the facade and owing little to classical precedent. The panels beneath the windows are set back and emphasize the columns, height, and frame construction. Figuratively and literally, the pilasters support the decorated frieze and the overhanging roof.

Sullivan's fame extended his practice throughout the United States. His Guaranty Building in Buffalo is similar to the Wainwright, but is thirteen stories tall. Here, the columns are integrated with the corniced roof in an elegant decorated curve. In Chicago, Sullivan also designed the Stock Exchange Building (1993–1894) and, finally, the much-loved Carson, Pirie, Scott department store (1898–1904), on twelve floors, with disciplined geometric facades and minimal decoration used to highlight the doorways and store windows. The horizontal and vertical elements in the facade are given equal status, and the resulting grid effect seems modern even today.

LEFT: The Wainwright Building (St. Louis, Missouri, 1891) demonstrated to the world the new vertical style that became the forerunner of the American skyscraper.

RIGHT: Louis Sullivan's Guaranty Building (Buffalo, 1896) uses vertical piers to create a sweeping sense of height, and unifies structure and ornamentation through beautifully-wrought spandrels and richly decorated windows.

CHAPTER TWO

THE HEYDAY OF THE AMERICAN SKYSCRAPER

The progress of skyscraper technology has always been a series of advances and restrictions. No sooner had the solution to one technical problem allowed a leap upwards, than it was halted by another constraint, until this too was overcome or bypassed. Hindsight makes some technological advances look simple and obvious which, at the time, seemed obscure or downright risky. It may now seem strange that it was not until twenty-five years after the construction of the Eiffel Tower that buildings actually designed for people to work in were built to the same scale. But conversely, after centuries of being vertically constrained, it is extraordinary that architects and engineers developed such tall skyscrapers so soon after Eiffel's pioneering efforts.

The responsibilities were awesome. Eiffel's structure had no real function, other than to impress—it was not a building meant to be occupied. On the other hand, failure or damage to

ABOVE: Early New York skyscrapers were built on bedrock, and this period aerial view of downtown Manhattan—showing tall buildings clustered at the lower part of the island—provides both a geological and an architectural overview of the island.

LEFT: Viewed end on, with a depth at the apex of only 6 feet (1.8 meters), the Flatiron Building appears to be almost like a wall.

any of the technically complicated components of a real sky-scraper could lead to potential catastrophe. Yet, spurred on by high land values and returns, not to mention corporate pride and ambition, architects and entrepreneurs accepted the challenge of learning how to build high, each improving on the achievements of his predecessors.

1900: The Search for a Style

At 285 feet (87 meters), the Flatiron Building—New York's first skyscraper—(Burnham and Root, 1903) caused almost as much excitement in New York as the Eiffel Tower had in Paris fifteen years earlier. The building sits on a thin, triangular plot, which it fills like a giant wedge of cheese, or the eponymous flatiron. Viewed end on, with a depth at its apex of only 6 feet (1.8 meters), the building appears to be almost like a wall, for at that angle it is without depth.

New Yorkers took much pride in this addition to their city, and the building gained an additional following from male gawkers loitering at its base hoping for a glimpse of female petticoats exposed by the eddying gusts of wind, a feature for which the building also became renowned.

The familiar silhouette of New York as we know it today owes much to the city's unique geology. The sound, underlying bedrock that lies close to the surface in some parts of

Manhattan makes New York an ideal skyscraper city, allowing the rock to bear the heavy loads of tall buildings. Where such direct bearing was not possible, later engineers developed complex foundation techniques. Rafts—thick concrete pads extending into the ground over a wider area than the tower—reduced the pressure on the ground; friction piles were driven deep through many layers of subsoil; or the building was floated by removing a volume of soil in the basement of equivalent weight to the building.

In 1904, the year after the Flatiron Building was completed, a similar building, again triangular in plan form, was built in Times Square—the Times Building by Cyrus Eidlitz. At 362 feet (110 meters), it was considerably taller than the Flatiron Building, but lacked its insubstantially thin effect. Both buildings rose sheer to projecting eaves, perhaps following the exam-

LEFT: The Times Tower. Occupying the Times Square Plot between 42 and 43rd streets, this landmark of midtown Manhattan was the headquarters of *The New York Times* from 1906 to 1913.

LEFT: The Flatiron Building was New York's first skyscraper, and, in 1903, it caused almost as much excitement in New York as the Eiffel Tower had in Paris fifteen years before. Built on a thin, triangular plot, this classic steel-frame-constructed tower is wrapped in an intricate blanket of limestone blocks.

ABOVE: Modern engineering and construction techniques have made it possible to build almost any type of structure within the entire space available in Manhattan—thus today's magnificent skyline differs substantially from that of decades past.

ple of Sullivan's Wainwright Building; but the facades were decorated in a Beaux-Arts style, which did not really suit such tall elevations.

Beginning with the classical style demonstrated in Greek and Roman buildings, each successive age had found some new interpretation of this common language. All had had to apply it to buildings constrained by brick and stone techniques, which meant that even large palaces were much longer than they were high. The grammar of classical design breaks up long horizontal lines and masses with vertical divisions. A four-story-high facade would typically have, say, a central block, perhaps slightly forward of the rest, with flanking pavilions at the end of each wing, creating the impression of a group of five linked units rather than one endless facade. With devices such as giant free-standing columns further subdividing each block, a pleasing harmony could be achieved between vertical and horizontal elements. But no classically based architectural language could deal with a facade that was taller than it was wide.

The High and the Mighty

While Chicago led the way in skyscraper technology and was the domestic trading hub of America, New York was the gateway to the rest of the world, and a natural home for the great American corporations and institutions, who wanted big build-

ings—but were also stylistically conservative and attached to European traditions. Burnham's reversion to classicism in the Flatiron Building contrasts with the boldness of his Chicago Reliance Building and with Sullivan's work, which had broken free from historical precedent.

Ernest Flagg's Singer Tower (1907) is a huge leap upwards, to 600 feet (183 meters). This is a genuine tower, 65 feet (20 meters) square, widening at the top, giving it a greater emphasis and mass. Although it also follows French Renaissance styles, with a domed mansard roof, the decoration is austere and restrained, with a style that unifies the different elements.

The Singer Tower did not retain its height preeminence for long. In 1909, Napoleon Le Brun completed the 700-foot-tall (213-meter) tower addition to the Metropolitan Life Company Building. The architect denied that his design was based on the campanile of St. Mark's Cathedral in Venice, but the similarities are striking. The company itself was delighted to be linked to such an illustrious antecedent, to which the famous British art historian John Ruskin, then at the height of his influence, had paid fulsome tribute.

Competition for status was endemic to the American corporations. The company headquarters was a flagship, its

LEFT: Downtown Chicago is an eclectic mixture of old-fashioned and modern architectural elements. Here, a view of the Michigan Avenue Bridge, the Wrigley Building, and the Chicago River.

LEFT: The elegant columns and the entrance way of the old AT&T Building in New York.

RIGHT: Even early corporate office buildings such as the old AT&T Building, at 195 Broadway in New York City, served as powerful symbols of the world of business and finance.

RIGHT: New York's Woolworth Building under construction in 1912. The flag marks the completion of the iron framework structure, clearly visible in this photograph.

device of dividing a long facade into wings with pavilions is seen here in a tall building; the wing pavilions are double-size campanile replicas, with curving links of equal height, and are linked with balanced curves to a taller central block crowned with a "wedding cake" of tiered colonnades and domes.

Gothic Influences

Like many of his contemporaries, architect Cass Gilbert had been trained in Europe in the Beaux-Arts tradition. But he cast aside his training in the 792-foot-tall (241-meter) Woolworth Building (1910–1913), where he had the brilliant idea of developing Gothic motifs to complement the height of the skyscraper.

As perfected in Europe in the middle ages, this style balanced the lateral thrusts from stone vaulted roofs with a series of buttresses, often with external arches (flying buttresses) to absorb these lateral loads as high up the building as possible. As the stonemasons acquired confidence, they filled the space between the vertical columns of masonry with glazing. The great medieval churches seem to soar into the sky, often capped with pinnacles and flanked by towers.

The suitability of a Gothic model for a skyscraper became obvious as soon as Gilbert had tried it. The vertical white terracotta bands of the Woolworth Building, partly influenced by Sullivan, emphasize its height just as the masonry columns had accentuated the height of the churches. Individual floors are hardly noticeable; the eye is led smoothly upwards to a splendid pinnacled top. Even though the detail is lost from a distance, the building is so cleverly massed from all the limited nearby viewpoints that it still retains its vertical impact (near a building, fore-

height denoting modernity and success, but with conservative architectural detailing making a subconscious reference to more traditional values. Nowhere is this disparity more neatly illustrated than by the extraordinary Custom House Tower in Boston (Peabody and Stearns,1909–11). Here, the dome of a modest Palladian rotunda is replaced with another full-blown campanile; the two halves of the building simply fail to add up to a whole.

The search for a suitable classical expression is developed further in McKim, Mead and White's Municipal Building (New York, 1910–1913). In straddling Chambers Street it echoes the triumphal arches of ancient Rome. The classical

LEFT: The ceiling in the lobby of the Woolworth Building demonstrates its Gothic heritage in stunning detail.

RIGHT: Cass Gilbert's Gothic masterpiece, the Woolworth Building, was completed in 1913 and immediately captured the public eye with its soaring tower, rich ornaments, and dramatic presence.

LEFT: Throughout history, people have envisioned future cityscapes, and some of these early dreamers foresaw New York as a city of sky-scrapers—complete with overhead walkways, biplanes, a blimp, and marvelous Gothic architecture.

RIGHT: Until recent times, high-beam construction crews often worked without protective devices. Here, a Rockefeller Center construction crew takes a break on a high beam.

shortening can reduce the impression of its height). The base is a tall block of twenty-nine floors, U–shaped, with its court away from Broadway. The square tower is placed centrally in the Broadway facade, and there are two setbacks en route to the top.

The Woolworth Building was the most ambitious skyscraper of its era. It provided space for over ten thousand workers and had twenty-nine elevators, two of which traveled from ground level to the fifty-fourth floor. These were then the tallest vertical elevators in the world, exploiting the 1904 elevator development of gearless traction to provide faster and smoother travel. Internally, the lobbies and public parts of the building were richly detailed with golden mosaics covering the dome of the lobby and fine Gothic decoration around the elevator doors. The Woolworth Company naturally loved the building. It was instantly dubbed the "Cathedral of Commerce," and must be one of the very few buildings in the world to have been paid for in cash, without loans.

But although the New York architects had mastered the engineering and technology needed to build great skyscrapers, they had not followed Chicago's stylistic lead. Sullivan's ideal of an American architecture was still elusive.

Zoning Ordinances

The building boom in downtown Manhattan had been a developers' free-for-all; as much "built space" as possible was crammed onto each plot to secure the highest return on capital. By 1913, it had become commonplace for twenty-story buildings to occupy an entire block, with vertical facades from roof to pavement turn-ing the streets into dark, narrow canyons. Skyscrapers came to be seen by many as selfish and egotistical edifices, in some ways symbolizing the presence of the corporate powers.

When the Equitable Life Company Building rose thirty-nine floors sheer above the surrounding streets in 1915, the city authorities felt they had to blow the whistle. The zoning ordinance came into effect in 1916. It was now not the laws of gravity or technological impossibility that constrained the skyscraper, but man-made obstacles.

Limits were placed on skyscraper size and form by relating the total permissible floor space to the size of the plot, at a ratio of 12 to 1. For the future, a building with vertical walls, occupying the whole of its plot, was capped at twelve stories. If it occupied only half the plot, it could rise to twenty-four stories. There were no height controls on the central quarter of each plot, provided the other rules were followed.

The zoning laws were not intended to outlaw tall buildings. Skyscrapers had by now become an identity symbol not just for their corporate owners, but also for New York and the United States as a whole. They were America's unique contribution to building form.

The Golden Age

The 1920s saw the New York and Chicago skylines transformed. Architects and engineers had previously had to grapple with structural problems and architectural aesthetics; they now had the extra problem of working out what three-dimensional massing could maximize the space permitted by the plot ratio.

LEFT: NBC Studios, Rockefeller Center. Before the era of television, the western buildings which housed media and entertainment offices were known as Radio City.

LEFT: An Art-Deco mural from the central mall area above the ice-skating rink in Rockefeller Center.

RIGHT: The General Electric Building in Rockefeller Center, one of a vast complex of buildings in a mixed-use site between 48th and 51st streets and Fifth Avenue and the Avenue of the Americas in midtown Manhattan.

RIGHT: Rockefeller Center's famous statue of Atlas holding the world on his shoulders. A statue of Prometheus by Paul Manship graces the central fountain of the complex.

The building owners added one further requirement—that the form of the skyscraper should be a unique reflection of their corporate image. Reconciling these disparate demands cannot have been easy.

Most skyscrapers were constructed around a core containing elevators, stairs, and the vertical servicing for the building. It was here that the bracing and stiffness was provided to transfer wind loading to the ground (the self weight of the buildings was less of a problem). The core was surrounded by office space; the limit on the width of this band was about 25 feet (7.6 meters), to give reasonable daylight throughout with normal ceiling heights. The outer edges of the floors were supported by columns, either incorporated in or close to the external walls.

Horizontal wind loading naturally increased as buildings became taller. Despite improvements in steel technology—which would have theoretically permitted lighter, more efficient structures—engineers responded cautiously (but by later standards, these 1920s buildings were substantially overstructured). The taller the building, the greater the horizontal shear force—the sideways force on the columns—at ground level. This is resisted by the thickness of the building and the core. Since the shear force is reduced at higher levels (although the actual wind pressure may be greater), buildings needed to be broad at the base, and thinner above.

The zoning ordinances also tended to produce tall structures with a ziggurat or stepped-pyramid form, progressively narrowing in a series of cutbacks or setbacks, as typified in Raymond Hood's Daily News Building (New York, 1929–1931). These cutbacks frequently relate to the reduced size of the core in the upper part of the building, where fewer elevators and stairs, and less structural depth, were needed.

The zoning laws made a contribution to the characteristic cutback skyscraper form, and they also led to better streets and public spaces. Rockefeller Center (New York, Raymond Hood, et al., 1930–1933) observes the spirit as well as the letter of the law.

The site of the American Radiator Company Building (Hood and Fouilhoux, 1924) opposite Bryant Park allowed the rare chance of a full frontal view, and the building made the most of its modest height. It featured a floodlit, knobbled top of gold terra-cotta glowing in the dark, emphasized by the dark brickwork which was indistinguishable from the windows even by day. The vertically ribbed form may owe something to the Woolworth Building, but it also makes a reference to the company name. The Palmolive Building in Chicago (Holabird and Roche, 1929) was nicknamed the "Cathedral of Cleanliness"; the top of New York's RCA Victor Building (Cross and Cross, 1931) was sculpted into an array of features emblematic of the company's products.

LEFT: From rooftop terraces to an underground shopping concourse, Rockefeller Center is a miniature city itself set within an urban fabric.

The Tribune Tower

Such imagery, which often attempted to work at a subconscious level, naturally had to relate to the architectural style of the building. Cass Gilbert's discovery of Gothic as a suitable clothing for skyscrapers was influential. At first, the Gothic style was followed literally, as in the winning design for the Chicago Tribune Building in 1922 (subsequently completed in 1925) by Hood and Howells. This was the first major work by Raymond Hood, who was to dominate skyscraper design for the next ten years.

The Tribune Tower drew inspiration from the medieval Butter Tower at Rouen; the top is progressively cut back to octagonal form with an exuberant display of pinnacles and flying buttresses. The friezes to the windows at street level have obvious origins in church roof screens and impressed the style of the building on even the busiest passerby.

There was an element of pastiche in this (as there had been in Le Brun's Metropolitan Life Tower of 1909) which was heavily criticized at the time. Indeed, the more restrained and generally preferred entry (which won second place in the competition) was by a Finn, Eliel Saarinen. This design was also Gothic influenced, but in a less literal and gimmicky way, with strong vertical emphasis, and cutbacks reflecting zoning requirements. Although never built, Saarinen's design became a blueprint of the ideal skyscraper for the next decade and beyond; encouraged by his reception, Saarinen emigrated to America shortly afterwards and started a large and successful practice.

John Howell's Panhellenic House reduces the Gothic references still further and is almost abstract and modernistic, exemplifying the skyscraper of the late 1920s. Hood's Daily News Building retains the Woolworth vertical features but eliminates the Gothic—only seven years after the Chicago Tribune competition. In many cases, of course, the Gothic style would not have conveyed the right message, as William van Alen's 1929 Chrysler Building demonstrates in its search for a corporate image—the building as logo. Both inside and out it is abstract, but also highly suggestive. The upper parts of the tower are skillfully cut back and unified into the extraordinary roof, a series of stainless-steel-clad arches, with triangular windows framed by neon. Exuberant and expressionistic, it was also memorable.

Sullivan had developed a style of flat facades, with smooth decoration related to and growing out of the form and structure of each building. The further development of this style in the 1920s came to be known as Art Deco. Sloan and Robertson's Chanin Building (1929) is one of the best examples of Art-Deco architecture. Inside and out, from window friezes to radiator grilles, the whole building is a continuum of flat, inlaid decoration.

RIGHT: Chicago's Tribune Tower (1930). Architects John Mead Howells and Raymond M. Hood won the *Tribune's* international competition "to secure for Chicago the most beautiful office building in the world."

LEFT: New York's extravagantly Art-Deco Chrysler Building exhibits the characteristic energy and drive of its era in both interior and exterior design

ABOVE: The elevator bank in the Chrysler Building shows the incredible attention to ornament and detail typical of this structure both inside and out.

ABOVE: Even the doors of the elevators in the classic Chrysler Building are Art-Deco masterpieces richly inlaid with cherry wood.

LEFT: This view of the jewel-like facade of the Chrysler Building shows the famous gargoyles posted on the corners.

ABOVE: Raymond Hood's McGraw-Hill Building (1929) is typical of the second period of skyscraper development in Manhattan, an era which is defined from the Singer Tower (1907) to Rockefeller Center (1931).

BELOW: A period view of New York's Empire State Building and surrounding skyscrapers, at the time when it was known as the tallest building in the world.

Beyond Decoration

Thus, two trends run side by side—Art Deco, and an increasingly severe, undecorated style, in which the building relies on materials and massing to make its statement. Rockefeller Center was faced with austere white/gray limestone slabs and gray aluminum, its effectiveness depending solely on the sleek form and finely chiseled cutbacks. The McGraw-Hill Building (also by Hood) similarly relies on stepped-form massing. The walls are flat, almost skinlike, the only relief coming from the greenish banded terra-cotta defining each floor. Lescaze and Howe's Philadelphia Savings Fund Society Building (1931–1932) is an even more uncompromising, precocious example of the undecorated International style—increasingly popular in Europe—translated into a tower block.

America took a great national pride in its growing collection of record-breaking buildings. Companies and their architects often engaged in fierce and sometimes acrimonious rivalry, such as that between William Van Alen, architect of the Chrysler Building, and H. C. Severence, responsible for the nearby Manhattan Bank Building.

The Chrysler Building had been designed to be the tallest in the world, but Severence altered the Manhattan Building by adding extra stories to make it taller. Van Alen, in response, had a tall spire secretly constructed in the elevator shaft of his build-

RIGHT: An aerial view of the Empire State Building. On a clear day it is possible to observe an area with a circumference of nearly 200 miles (320 kilometers) from the highest observation tower.

RIGHT: Frank Lloyd Wright's Johnson Wax Administration Building (1938) has a sleek, streamlined exterior enclosing a magical, curving interior space.

BELOW: Plan, elevation, and section for the Johnson Wax Administration Building and Research Laboratory Tower in Racine, Wisconsin.

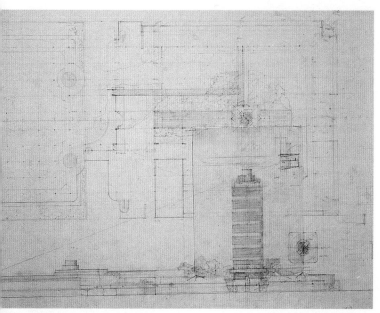

LEFT: New York's Radio City Music Hall (completed in 1932) under construction. Designed by Peter Clark using the principle of acoustic arches, this immense auditorium seats up to six thousand people.

ing, and waited until the bank had been topped out and completed; the spire was then triumphantly bolted into position to claim the height record at 1,046 feet (319 meters).

Two days after the completion of the Chrysler Building, Wall Street crashed. The skyscraper era was over, although projects already under construction, such as the Philadelphia Savings Fund Society Building and Rockefeller Center, were finished. Among these was the Empire State Building (Shreve, Lamb, and Harmon, 1930–1931). Watching this building go up at record speed gave New Yorkers hope of better times ahead. Its massive steel frame was designed to take 6,000 tons of wind loading—its sway in a wind is negligible. The building even withstood an aircraft collision in 1945 without structural damage. At 1,250 feet (381 meters), the Empire State Building took the height record and retained it until 1977— longer than any other skyscraper. Despite the Depression it was finished in the usual lavish style, with inlaid, marble floors and foyers (the costs of labor and materials halved in the years when it was being built). The Empire State Building was a speculative venture, and when it was finished the office space was unwanted, earning it the satirical title of the "Empty State Building."

The Depression and the second world war effectively halted skyscraper building for twenty years. But in 1936, Frank Lloyd Wright, the doyen of American architects, built a small building in Racine, Wisconsin. It looked as if it had been poured as liquid into a round-cornered mold to set in layers, first pink-brown, then clear, in bands repeated to the top. This was the headquarters of the Johnson Wax Company. This remarkable piece of corporate imagery is achieved by the form of the

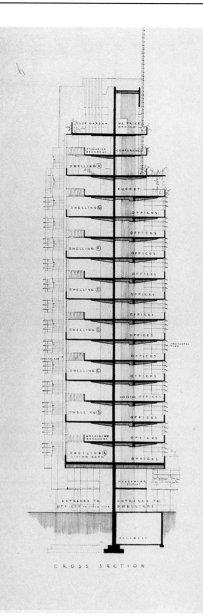

CROSS SECTION

RIGHT: Cross-section of the H. C. Price Company Tower in Bartlesville, Oklahoma. An early example of mixed-use design, Frank Lloyd Wright's tower combined office units and apartments in a dramatic vertical interior space.

RIGHT: Typical floor plan of the H. C. Price Company Tower (1952–1956).

LEFT: Wright's H. C. Price Company Tower (Bartlesville, Oklahoma, 1956) is a nineteen-story tower that, although originally designed for Manhattan, still manages to look small, even in the environs of a Western city.

building alone, without any additional decoration.

The Johnson Wax Administration Building looked forward in two ways. First, in the use of concrete, of which Wright was a great pioneer. (His early cantilevered designs seemed so daring that the workmen refused to remove the shuttering in which the concrete had been cast.) The building cantilevers the floor slabs off a central core, and, in a second daring innovation, the outside walls—essentially made of glass—are suspended from the floors, fulfilling Jenney's 1880s prophecy of curtain walls. It is the resulting lack of structure in the surface membrane that gives it the smooth, waxy appearance.

Wright also designed a small skyscraper in the late 1930s, although this was not built and finished until 1953. The Price Tower, in Bartlesville, Oklahoma, did not achieve its proper place among the earliest of the reinforced-concrete skyscrapers, but its sculpted facades were to influence other architects even before it had been built.

But by 1953 the world had changed, and so had the form of the skyscraper.

LEFT: Mile High Illinois was Wright's plan for a mile-high sky-scraper in Chicago. This unrealized plan for a glass-curtained tower uses a deep tap root core to anchor the building to the ground.

ABOVE: The state capitol building, Lincoln, Nebraska (1922-1932). This is one of the later buildings designed by Bertrand Goodhue, whose work exhibited a Gothic influence joined with a sensativity for contemporary construction techniques.

CHAPTER THREE

EUROPEAN SKYSCRAPERS AND THE INTERNATIONAL STYLE

The first world war marked the end of the old order in Europe. The postwar years were a time of intense architectural exploration—of new materials and structural principles, of new building forms and styles. This time saw the gradual eclipse of the classical Beaux-Arts and Gothic traditions.

Mendelssohn's expressionistic Einstein Tower at Potsdam (1913) and the drawings of futuristic cities by Chiattone (1914) and St. Elia (1917) sowed seeds which eventually bore fruit: the modernism of Le Corbusier, who essentially explored the sculptural qualities of concrete, and the International style of Mies van der Rohe, based on precise and correct detailing of materials. Both ideals eschewed all forms of decoration—this was felt to detract from the inherent beauty of the building form. These architects believed that a building's function should dictate both its internal organization and form, which should not, therefore, be arbitrarily imposed.

European architects paid little attention to the skyscraper form. Eugen Schmohl's Borsigturm (Berlin, 1922), and the

Tagblatt House by Ernst Osswald (Stuttgart, 1924) are two small, early examples notable for their austere styling. In the 1920s, few Europeans were looking to America for a cultural lead—the traffic in ideas had always run from East to West.

However, by the 1930s Le Corbusier was advocating the widespread use of tall buildings, even for housing. The advantages, as he saw them, included rationalization of journeys and reduction of traffic; the freeing of open space at ground level for recreation and enjoyment; and greater privacy and independence for the occupants.

In Germany and Italy progressive architecture was not considered politically sound, and Mies van der Rohe and Walter Gropius emigrated to the United States, where they were both to strongly influence the form of the postwar skyscraper. And it was not until after the end of the second world war that Le Corbusier's theories were put into practice.

Concrete

The Romans had used concrete extensively, but their secrets had been lost until the nineteenth century. In the 1930s, progressive architects such as Wright and Le Corbusier realized concrete's outstanding structural and sculptural qualities.

Concrete is mixed as a liquid, and then poured into a mold or shutter (generally of wood) where it sets; the shuttering is then removed. It is strong in compression (as in a column), but weak in tension (if pulled apart); but nineteenth- and twenti-

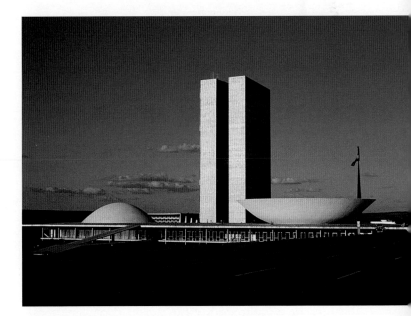

ABOVE: Brasilia, the federal district of Brazil designed by Lucio Costa, is a monumental city that was specifically created to achieve a redistribution of power and wealth as well as to open the interior of the country for development.

LEFT: La Defense, the business district of Paris. Specially constructed on a site away from any historic buildings, this complex gave free rein to innovation in design.

LEFT: In structures such as the
Centrepoint Building, London
(1963), the designer has been able
to give a deep, faceted, or rough
texture to the building facade.

The problem with concrete
has traditionally been setting
time. Only a limited amount
can be poured at a time, and
the layer below has to be
hardened sufficiently to carry
the load of the one above.
Many attempts have been
made to overcome this problem, which slows the con-
struction process and increas-
es costs. One answer has been
to precast the concrete off
site. The fully hardened components can be as large as
cranes can handle. Some
buildings have been almost
entirely prefabricated.

The other approach has
been to use additives to the
concrete mix to speed up the
drying, but those used in the
1950s and 1960s have been
found to decay. Advances in
technology are now making it
possible to cast concrete with slip-form shuttering rising at a
rate to match the curing time, so that the concrete can be
poured continuously.

Often these components are strongest if they have a molded,
three-dimensional form, and the designer is able to give a deep,
faceted, or rough texture to the building facade, as at
Centrepoint in London (Seifert, 1963). He is also free to use the
concrete only as a frame, with perhaps all-glass facades; indeed,
it is not always obvious whether a particular structure is made
of steel or concrete.

The Pirelli Building in Milan (Gio Ponti and Nervi, 1958) is
one of the most arresting tall structures in Europe—its taper-

eth-century engineers developed a system of adding reinforcement in the form of steel bars or mesh, which increased the tensile strength. In the 1960s, it became possible to pre-tension the
steel wires in the shutter, inducing a stress in the concrete opposite to that it was to carry. Despite the steel's greater tension, the
concrete could now carry extra loading before it became over-
stressed.

Because the reinforcement could extend in all directions,
floor slabs could span in more than one direction and complex
cantilevers were easily achieved, as Wright demonstrated.
Concrete can also be cast into virtually any shape for which
shuttering can be devised—a boon for an imaginative designer.

ing ends and defined top recall New York's Flatiron Building. But the ingenious concrete structure is not evident externally; it is concealed by the bland curtain walling then in vogue.

High-Rise Housing

After 1945 the priority of Europe was to rebuild—fast. Cities were flattened over much of the continent. Social reconstruction was also a priority; the high unemployment that had spawned the disasters of fascism was not to be allowed to return. Architecture was seen as one of the ways of achieving this brave new world.

With whole communities flattened by bombing, the theories of Le Corbusier became very persuasive. Tall housing blocks—vertical garden cities—set pleasantly in parkland, were an advance on the small, back-to-back houses and narrow, crowded streets they were replacing.

The Unité d'Habitation, the first prototype of Le Corbusier's ideal, was built amid howls of protest in 1947 near Marseilles,

ABOVE: The lobby of Trump Tower, one of Manhattan's vertical luxury shopping centers.

LEFT: The glamor of New York's Fifth Avenue is reflected in Trump Tower (1983), designed by Swanke, Hayden, Connell and Partners as a mixed-used building containing both retail shopping and residential apartments.

in a heroic all-concrete style later to be known as brutalism. It was widely copied throughout Europe.

The profile of the city was changed by these blocks. People living in the center were frequently relocated to new slab blocks on the outskirts, only to find later that their old homes had been replaced with commercial and office buildings. While the central areas were often rebuilt precisely in their original form (even replicating whole buildings) to preserve their heritage (or with new buildings which respected their context), the outskirts were full of strange, tall slabs—unlike American cities, where tall buildings reflected the high capital and rental values in downtown locations.

In England, new housing meant more votes for the political parties; the 1960s saw a scramble to build. Building taller gave more space at relatively little extra expense, so taller and cheaper housing towers were erected. Goldfinger's Trellick Tower (1968) in North Kensington, London, is a fine piece of architecture, but in England, buildings of this sort have proved to be disastrous as housing. "Tower block" has become a term of abuse, and concrete a hated material.

But when well designed, well managed, and lived in by people who have chosen to be there, skyscrapers in Britain, such as the Barbican development in London (Chamberlain, Powell and Bon, 1950s–1970s), as well elsewhere in Europe—where there is less antipathy to high-rise living—can and do deliver at least part of the Le Corbusier dream. Chicago's Marina City, in concrete, described as "two corn cobs" (Bertrand Goldberg, 1967) and the steel-framed Lake Shore Drive Apartments (Mies van der Rohe, 1948–1951) illustrate this in a city with a strong predilection for the skyscraper.

The International Style

How far and fast Le Corbusier's ideals spread is illustrated by Oscar Niemaye's copybook interpretation of his ideals in the government buildings in Rio de Janeiro (1947). The United Nations Building in New York (Harrison and Abramovitz, et. al., 1947–1953) showed the direct result of his influence—it is a plain, unadorned slab rising thirty-nine floors. Its green-glazed long walls facing east and west proved incompatible with the air conditioning system—but they still set a trend. Gone was the world of expressionism and Art Deco. These towers marked the beginning of the International style—clean, simple volumetric forms; regular, repeated units giving order to the elevations; restrained detailing; and an absence of decoration.

No building expresses this ideal more straightforwardly than Lever House in New York (Skidmore, Owings and Merrill, 1950–1952). A low block with a low roofline covers the plot, giving continuity and emphasis to the street. Rising quite separately above this is a smooth, glass-clad slab block, with its narrow end onto the street, again reducing its impact. The regularity of the cladding is possible because the frame is hidden. As in Wright's Johnson Wax Administration Building, the external curtain walls seem to be weightless. Each elevational bay is divided into three: the window, a green obscured glass panel below it, and a third panel concealing the structural depth of the

LEFT: United Nations Headquarters, New York City. An international design effort inspired by the architectural precepts of Le Corbusier, this building reflects a desire for world peace and progress through world government.

ABOVE: New York's Seagram Building (1954–1958) is sheathed in bronze curtain walls, with a special finish designed by architect Mies van der Rohe.

LEFT: Marina City in Chicago (1963) is a dramatically situated mixed-used complex consisting of two central towers rising from a two-story base set on the Chicago River.

FOLLOWING PAGE:
The Singapore skyline at night. The architectural and urban situation in Singapore is rich and full of potential.

floor slabs, the horizontal services distribution, and the full air conditioning systems now installed.

The International style is attributed to Mies van der Rohe, who was certainly influential in its evolution. His Lake Shore Drive Apartments exhibit all the bland urbane manners of the style, and are a classic example of the genre. Mies's later Seagram Building (New York, 1954–1958), raised on columns forming a plaza at ground level, following Rockefeller Center's example (and Le Corbusier's dictates), is generally felt to perfect the style.

The International style found international uses: Arne Jakobsen's SAS Building (Copenhagen, 1958) uses the Lever House scheme, with the airline occupying the lower slab and a hotel the upper one. Heinrich and Petschnigg's Phoenix–Rheinrohr AG Building (Dusseldorf, 1955–1960) suggests, however, that even at the time this extreme simplicity was found too obvious. Here the twenty-two-floor-tower is subdivided into three more or less equal vertical slices which are set back horizontally and vertically, recalling the zoning law effects. Later designers were to return to the idea of adding interest by massing buildings in a more complex way.

Eero Saarinen's CBS Building (New York, 1960–1964) recalls the vertical emphasis of such 1920s skyscrapers as Panhellenic House. A series of V-shaped vertical ribs and grooves running straight from top to bottom have replaced the gridded curtain walls. These do not pretend to be structural; they create a clean, meticulously detailed grille with an ever-changing balance of light and shade.

All subsequent designers were to take the International style of Mies and his followers as their starting point—even if the end results were quite different. Lake Point Tower in Chicago (Schipporeit and Heinrich, 1968–1969) brings together many of the strands of the previous two decades. It is inspired by Mies's glass tower proposal (1920–1921); and the smooth curtain-wall facades are actually rounded and flow like a curtain, recalling the Johnson Wax AdministrationBuilding.

The logical development of the International style was to remove all evidence of the framing components from the facade. H. N. Cobb and I. M. Pei's John Hancock Tower in Boston, sixty stories tall, hides not just its main structure from public view, but also all the bolts and braces of the facade itself—it is a succession of mirrored glass plates. At a low level the building reflects its surroundings, at the upper level it reflects the sky. Is the John Hancock Tower an answer to the problem of context? It stands in startling contrast to its neighbor, H. H. Richardson's century-old Romanesque-revival church. The only concessions to visual interest are small indents in the two shorter elevations which reflect the building's rhomboidal plan.

Skyscrapers of Today

By the mid-1960s, the 102 floors of the Empire State Building had stood supreme for thirty years. It was then estimated that the building contained at least twice as much steel as was structurally necessary. New, stronger steels had evolved in the 1950s, and for any given core size—determined by elevator and staircase requirements—buildings could now be taller.

In the 1920s, the core had been the obvious place for the bracing members transferring the wind loading to the ground, and the stepback form, with a larger base narrowing as the tower rose, was a direct expression of the relationship between wind loading and plan area. The Transamerica Tower in San Francisco (William Pereira, 1972) is even more diagrammatic—it is a simple pyramid.

Tall buildings cause winds to eddy in strange and unpredictable ways, and differential pressure can be disastrous if windows are opened. Fully developed air conditioning systems have

ABOVE: A view of downtown Seattle at sunset. Each city's unique skyline is a recognizable and potent symbol of its presence in the world.

LEFT: Downtown San Francisco features the Transamerica Corporation's pyramid-shaped headquarters, about which the *San Francisco Examiner* wrote in 1973: "Transamerica is getting more than architectural attention. It's winning identification along with San Francisco."

now acclimatized people to working in a sealed environment. While daylight requirements limited the width of a tower from its windows to the core, a completely internal environment imposes no such restrictions. Buildings became much broader, with windows merely providing visual contact with the outside world.

If the wind resistance strength of a tall structure is related to the diameter of its core, then the strongest structure will be the one with the widest core. The logical next step was therefore to abolish the core, and to take the loading back on to the external walls—the whole building, in effect, becoming the core. The extra width gained in this fashion gives much greater height potential to the design.

This is an about-face on eighty years of skyscraper evolution, and completely overthrows Jenney's idea of removing the load-

LEFT: The Frankfurt skyline offers an astonishing blend of the old and the new, including the buildings of the Westend-strasse complex, which provide office space for the headquarters of the DG Bank.

OPPOSITE: Westendstrasse I (1993, architect William Pedersen) is set on the Mainzer Landstrasse in the very heart of Frankfurt's banking center. The complex, which includes a 52-story tower and smaller buildings, offers business, residential, and retail space. The dramatically cantilevered steel crown of the tower points toward the historic center of old Frankfurt, and has become a part of that city's signature skyline.

ABOVE: Frankfurt has been a center of commerce from the earliest moments in European history, and its architecture reflects a diversity of interests and eras. Here, the adjacent BFG and Mercedes buildings provide a study in contrasting styles.

ABOVE: At 850 feet (259 meters), Frankfurt's Messeturm is the tallest commercial building in Europe. Designed by Chicago architect Helmut Jahn, this 55-story structure is ornamented with red granite and topped with a pyramid.

RIGHT: The Time-Life Building (1960) in New York is a classic example of the 1950s and 1960s post-Miesian skyscraper which offers functionality and quiet elegance.

LEFT: The Sears Tower in Chicago is currently the tallest building in the world. To the right can be seen the office building at 311 South Wacker Drive, and in the foreground is the South branch of the Chicago River.

bearing function from the external walls. Although elevators and escape stairs are still required, the elimination of a core creates more usable space. Improved fire protection materials, smoke and fire detection devices, and sprinkler controls have all contributed to the next generation of bigger and taller forms.

A true expression of this approach will show the necessary framing externally. The John Hancock Center in Chicago (Bruce Graham, with Skidmore, Owings and Merrill, 1970) demonstrates this bold approach, and required about half the amount of structural steel needed for a skyscraper of equivalent size in the 1930s. The World Trade Center in New York (Minomi Yamasaki with Emery Roth, 1973–1976) at last toppled the supremacy of the Empire State Building using this

new all-core approach. The twin towers of the World Trade Center rise 110 floors to 1,350 feet (411 meters). It has to be said that the buildings are rather dull, with no expression of volume or form, or of the external core structure. All interest for the viewer has gone—the buildings are virtually without scale.

With the record at stake, it seemed for a while that New York might see a repeat of the inter-war-years rivalry between building owners and architects. The Empire State Building considered adding fifteen floors to win the record back from both the World Trade Center and the nearly contemporary Sears Tower in Chicago (Bruce Graham, with Skidmore, Owings and Merrill, 1974), which at 1,450 feet (442 meters) and 114 floors, took the record from the World Trade Center.

TOP RIGHT: A stunning bronze sculpture by Fritz Koenig is the centerpiece of the plaza in front of the World Trade Center.

RIGHT: Concerts and other cultural events are held in the Winter Garden, the glass-roofed atrium linking the twin towers of the World Financial Center.

LEFT: The enormous twin towers of the World Trade Center, viewed from the waters of New York harbor.

New Forms of Expression

The World Trade Center might be twin towers, but the Sears Tower is a body of nine parts, although the division is only a structural one—it is a set of nine separate coreless tubes, each with an external structure. These tubes rise irregularly to different heights, perhaps making faint references back to the ancient ziggurats. Elevators must travel at 20 miles per hour (32 kilometers per hour) to reach the upper floors.

As well as seeking height and maximum leaseable space, architects have explored more expressive forms. The Phoenix–Rheinrohr Building and Boston's John Hancock Center have facades massed in a more complicated way than was strictly essential. At Lake Shore Drive, Mies had invented the twin form—the two blocks at right angles give the viewer a simultaneous double vision.

Peter and Alison Smithson's Economist Building (London, 1963–1867) had shown how grouped buildings could be integrated into the city fabric and offer a series of altering views and silhouettes. Similarly, the World Trade Center is partly redeemed by its changing silhouette. In the 1970s this approach became increasingly fashionable—Saarinen's partners Roche and

Dinkeloo built twin towers at the UN Plaza (1976). While the facades are impassive grids, the odd corner is sliced off, or buttressed, and the tension is increased because the towers are not identical.

Philip Johnson and John Burgee's Pennzoil Place (Houston, 1976) is almost Siamese-twin towers, and looks so from most viewpoints. The minimal gap between the buildings is intend-ed to look uncomfortable, and the sloping roofs and atrium add to the complexity of the form.

With such use of angles, chopped-off corners, and sloping roofs, these buildings are reacting against the bland, impersonal formula of matchbox forms of the earlier postwar skyscrapers. Johnson and Burgee's American Telephone and Telegraph Company Building (New York, 1984) is the first

LEFT: AT&T Corporate Headquarters, New York. At the time of planning for this company showpiece, AT&T's chairman told the architects, "I simply want the finest building in the world."

RIGHT: The classic 333 South Wacker Drive office tower (Kohn Pedersen Fox, architects) is a fine example of "literal functionalism" in design.

postmodern skyscraper—a reinterpretation of the triumphal arch and the classical broken pediment. Its masonry-clad walls make another break with tradition. Two later buildings by the same architects, PPG (Pittsburgh Plate Glass) Place (1984) and the Houston Republican Bank (1981–1984) also refer back to past examples.

PPG Place is a reworking of the classic setback skyscraper of the 1930s, inspired by Eliel Saarinen's 1922 Chicago Tribune design. Of course, it is all glass, and the historical reference is complete, the Gothic verticality implying a "cathedral of glass."

The Houston Bank has a similar elevational treatment, but the form here seems more arbitrary; 333 Walker Drive, Chicago (Koln Pedersen Fox, 1982) also explores an alternative form combined with smooth curtain-wall facades.

More innovative in its break with traditional forms and elevational treatment is Richard Roger's Lloyd's Building in London (1985). While not large by skyscraper standards, it is interesting that it turns the normal components of a tall building inside out. Instead of being in a core, all the services and elevators are externally sited, leaving the floor areas free and open, a freedom

ABOVE: The spectacular glass-roofed atrium of the Lloyd's Building in London's financial district rises to a height of twelve stories.

RIGHT: The interior of the Lloyd's Building, which is organized as a series of superimposed, concentric gallery spaces overlooking the central atrium.

LEFT: An exterior view of the Lloyd's of London Building, an innovative structure that turns the normal components of a tall building inside out with all the services and elevators externally sited and the floor areas open and free.

exploited by the main hall rising through several floors. It is deliberately unlike the staid, conservative building that might have been expected from an underwriting institution.

Norman Foster's Hong Kong and Shanghai Bank (1985) wears its structure literally on the outside. Each of the four vertical leaves of the building is supported by pairs of columns, linked at intervals by huge beams. The floors are set inside these, and suspended from them in tiers. It is a unique structure, and its directness should prove a challenge and inspiration to the future.

BELOW: The Hong Kong & Shanghai Banking Corporation Building (1979–1985) articulates an architecture based on both innovative technology and Chinese traditions.

ABOVE: A dramatic view from Hong Kong Park, central district, showing a selection of skyscrapers, including the base of the Bank of China in the foreground.

LEFT: The Bank of China, Hong Kong (1990). This seventy-story crystalline structure is very close to that of the Hong Kong and Shanghai Bank. A bamboo motif throughout symbolizes growth and strength.

FOLLOWING PAGE:
The World Financial Center is part of Cesar Pelli's $1.5 billion Battery Park project, a mixed-use site including commercial space, retail shopping, recreation and exhibition space, and beautifully landscaped public parks and plazas overlooking the harbor and the Statue of Liberty.

Where Now?

In the fifty years since the second world war skyscrapers have ceased to be a purely American phenomenon. They are now a worldwide building form and every continent has examples from 600 to 900 feet (180 to 275 meters) tall. Telecommunications requirements have pushed up skyscraper technology; these towers are now the highest in the world. Moscow's tower at 1,762 feet (537 meters) was exceeded by the CN Tower in Toronto (1975). A proposed tower in Jakarta will be even taller.

The downtown skylines for so long restricted to New York and Chicago are now ubiquitous. Skyscrapers are found in most American cities and increasingly dominate the skylines of Europe—the famous views of St. Paul's Cathedral are dwarfed by London's own complement of towers. They have sometimes been controversial additions to the cityscape, especially in Europe. Paris forbade skyscrapers until the 752-foot -tall (230-meter) Tour Maine–Montparnasse (1973); it is said to have been only President Pompidou's determination to modernize the city that reversed this policy. Britain now has the controversial Canary Wharf (Cesar Pelli/Koln Pedersen Fox, 1992), at 850 feet (259 meters) the tallest in Britain, dominating the Greenwich Meridian.

And Hong Kong, restricted for lateral places to grow, like Manhattan, has become a skyscraper city—though perhaps not quite according to Le Corbusier's ideal—with height equated with economic success and status. I. M. Pei and Henry Cobb's Bank of China, at 1,209 feet (369 meters) explores triangular geometry with the bundled-tube principle of the Sears Tower.

These tube structures have an immense strength, but their maximum height is related to the plan width or depth by a ratio limited at 6 or 7 to 1 by the remaining problem confronting engineers: that of sway. All tall buildings move—they are designed to allow this, for the strength of steel lies partly in its elasticity. The

RIGHT: A view looking upward through the tent-like roof of a structure in La Defense, Paris' ultra-modern financial center.

LEFT: The Grande Arche at La Defense could be called a modern-day interpretation of the Arc de Triomphe.

taller the building, or the greater its height-to-width ratio, the more it will move in the wind. It is alarming, to say the least, at a hundred floors up to see another building moving past the window; and as human beings are very sensitive to changes in speed and acceleration, the sway can even cause motion sickness. It is the physiology of people themselves that is now capping the race for height. Wright's 1953 proposal for a mile-high skyscraper is now quite feasible technically—but it can only usefully be built if techniques for mastering sway can be devised.

The story currently ends where it started—on the edge of Paris, just over a hundred years after Eiffel constructed his tower—where architects Jean Nouvel and Ove Arups are completing the design for a tower with a 10 to 1 height-to-width ratio, incorporating, as it must, a sway damping device. This is a 600-ton pendulum at the top, suspended in viscous silicon which absorbs the energy of the sway, reducing it by about half to 3 feet (1 meter)—an acceptable level for humans to work with. The 1,475 foot-tall (450 meter) tower is expected to be completed soon after the year 2000. As one of the first skyscrapers of the new millennium its name suitably sums up man's ambition to build tall; it is called the *"Tour sans Fin"*—the Endless Tower.

LEFT: An aerial view of Shinjuku, Tokyo.

ABOVE: Canary Wharf and Canary Wharf Tower, Docklands, Isle of Dogs, London. In times of economic uncertainty, developers often stumble over the completion of large developments such as that at Canary Wharf.

ABOVE: As cities such as Chicago add to their existing port-folio of architecture, new buildings such as the State of Illinois Center, need to be sufficiently memorable to stand out, and so are increasingly being given eccentric shapes.

OPPOSITE: Fluffy white clouds and a vivid blue sky are reflected in the towers of Frankfurt's Deutsche Bank, two ultra-modern buildings which not only reach for the sky, but blend into it.

INDEX